LOOK AND FIND®

Tonka®

Written by Kurt Hettinger
Illustrated by Art Mawhinney

Published by
Louis Weber, C.E.O.
Publications International, Ltd.
7373 North Cicero Avenue
Lincolnwood, Illinois 60712

Ground Floor, 59 Gloucester Place
London W1U 8JJ

www.pilbooks.com

Manufactured in China.

8 7 6 5 4 3 2 1

ISBN 1-4127-0535-5

publications international, ltd.

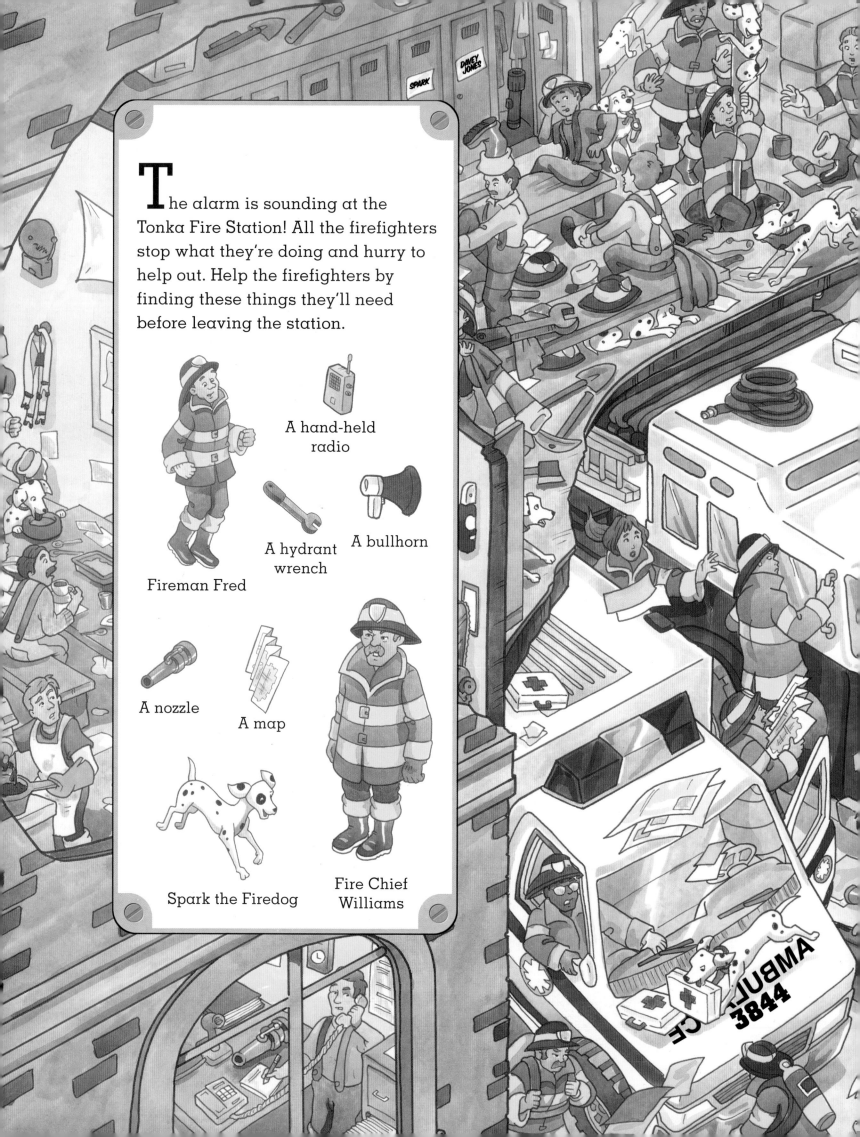

The alarm is sounding at the Tonka Fire Station! All the firefighters stop what they're doing and hurry to help out. Help the firefighters by finding these things they'll need before leaving the station.

A hand-held radio

A hydrant wrench

A bullhorn

Fireman Fred

A nozzle

A map

Spark the Firedog

Fire Chief Williams

Officer O'Malley and the other rookie police officers are completing their training on the driving courses. When they're finished, no getaway cars will be able to get away from them! Find O'Malley and the things he'll need to pass his tests today.

Keys

This motorcycle helmet

Handcuffs

Officer O'Malley

A utility belt

A police dispatch radio

A notepad and pencil

A spare tire

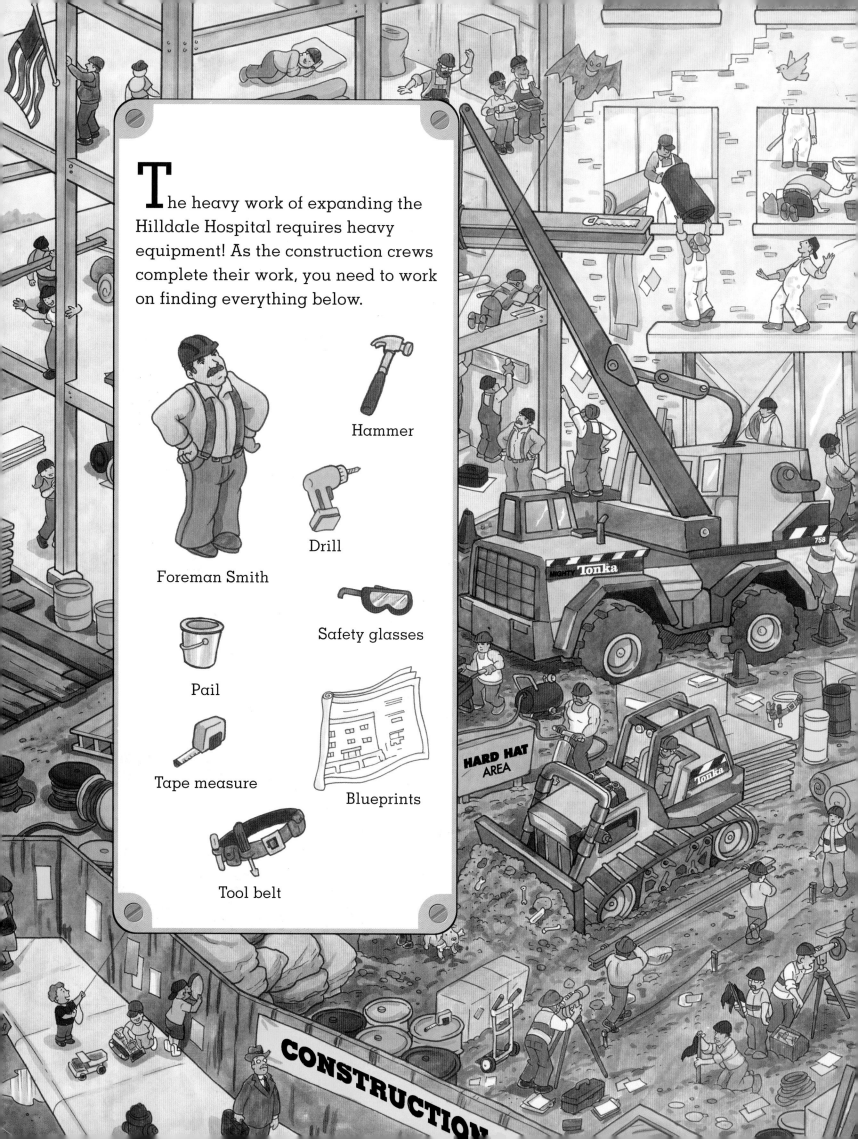

The heavy work of expanding the Hilldale Hospital requires heavy equipment! As the construction crews complete their work, you need to work on finding everything below.

Foreman Smith

Hammer

Drill

Safety glasses

Pail

Tape measure

Blueprints

Tool belt

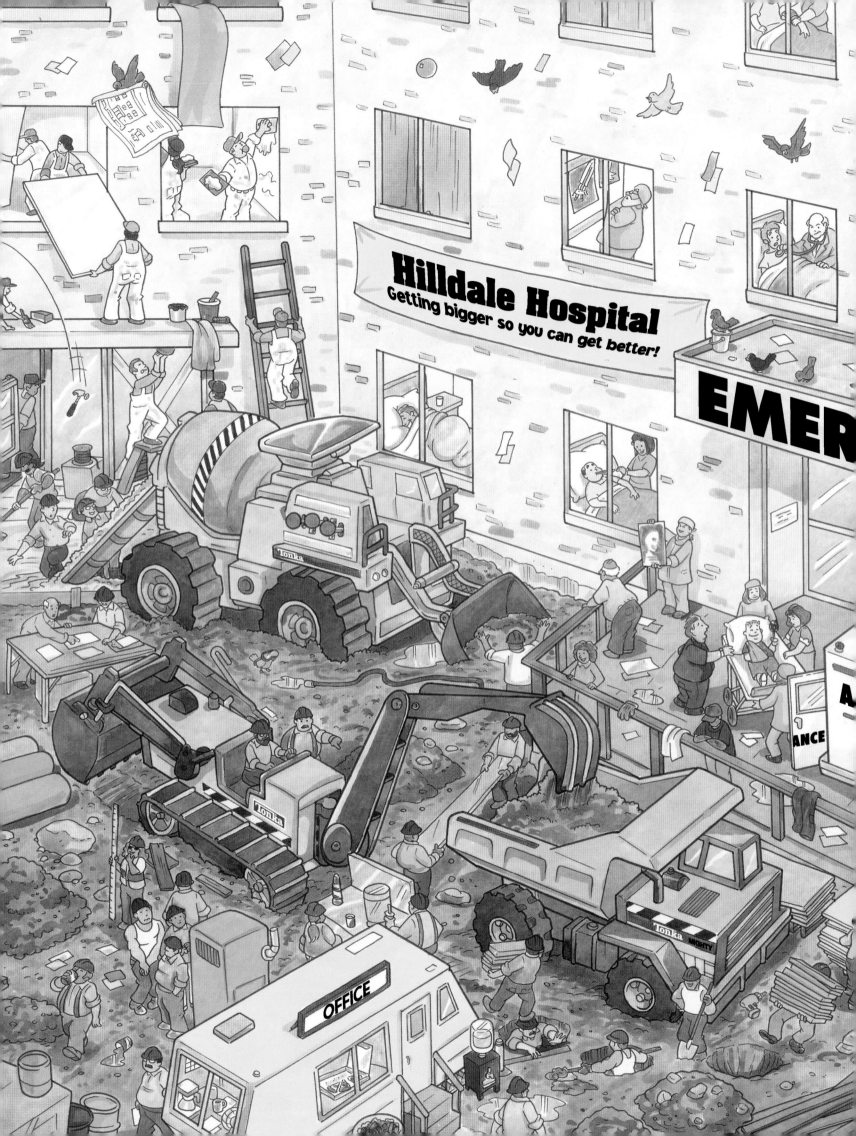

Today's the day for the big Air and Water Show, and everyone's out in style! Everything that can fly or float is showing off a bit today. Show off your finding skills by picking out some of our friends at the show.

Otto-Pilot
the Robot

Peg the Sea Dog

Pilot Jane

Gary
the Glider

Co-pilot Carl

Hovercraft
Harry

Captain Jack

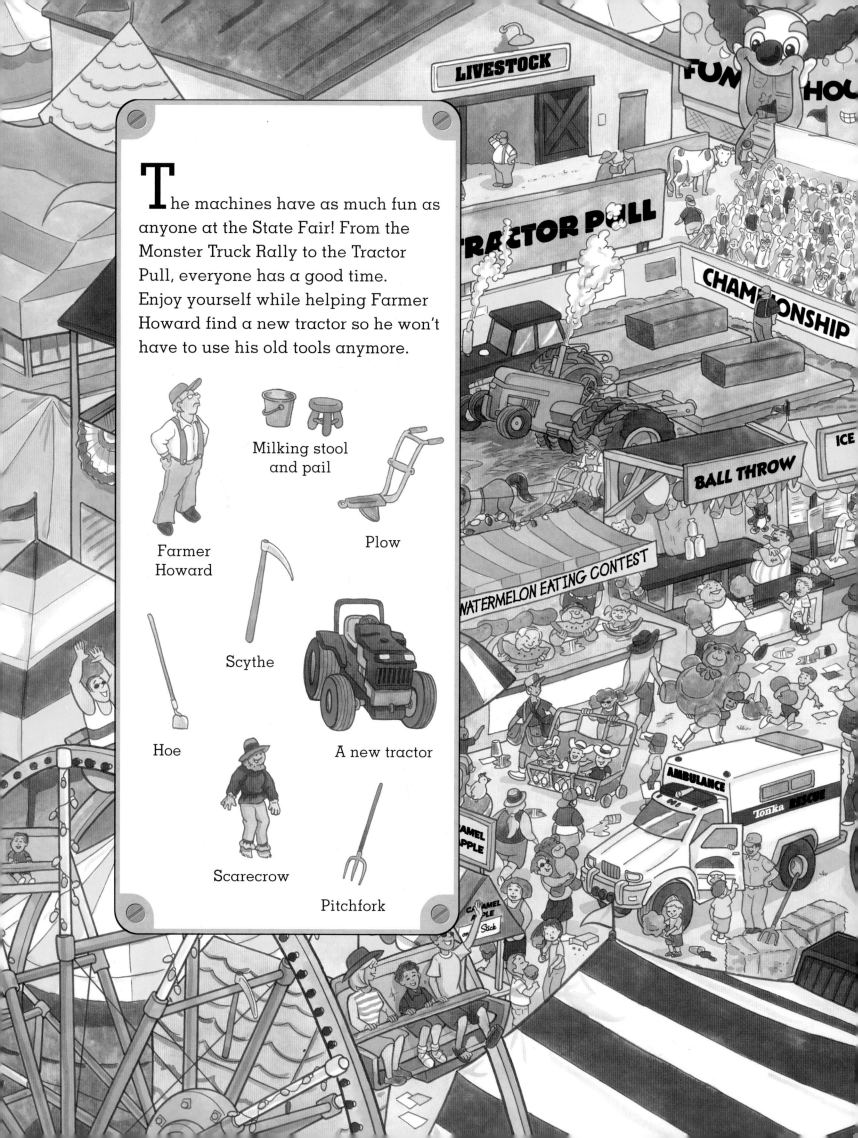

The machines have as much fun as anyone at the State Fair! From the Monster Truck Rally to the Tractor Pull, everyone has a good time. Enjoy yourself while helping Farmer Howard find a new tractor so he won't have to use his old tools anymore.

Farmer Howard

Milking stool and pail

Plow

Scythe

Hoe

A new tractor

Scarecrow

Pitchfork

LIVESTOCK

FUN HOU

TRACTOR PULL

CHAMPIONSHIP

ICE

BALL THROW

WATERMELON EATING CONTEST

AMBULANCE

Tonka RESCUE

CARAMEL APPLE

Stick

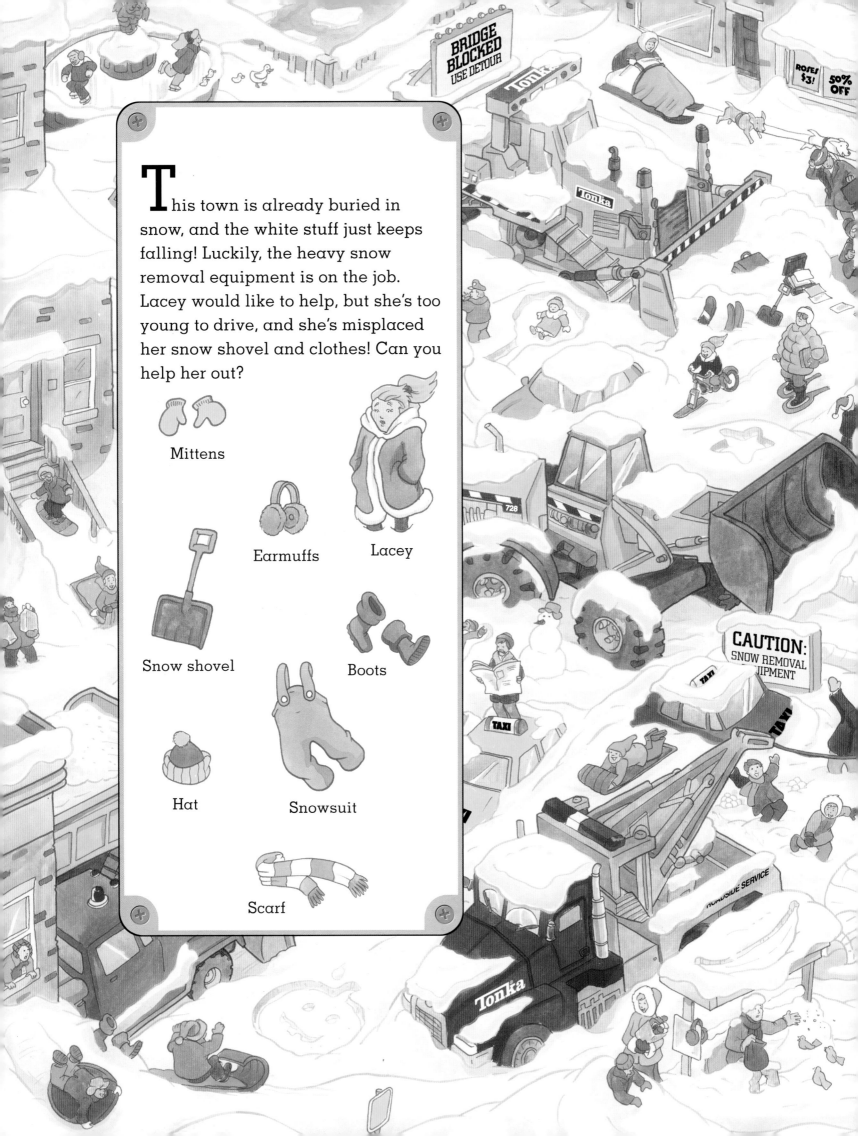

This town is already buried in snow, and the white stuff just keeps falling! Luckily, the heavy snow removal equipment is on the job. Lacey would like to help, but she's too young to drive, and she's misplaced her snow shovel and clothes! Can you help her out?

Mittens

Earmuffs

Lacey

Snow shovel

Boots

Hat

Snowsuit

Scarf

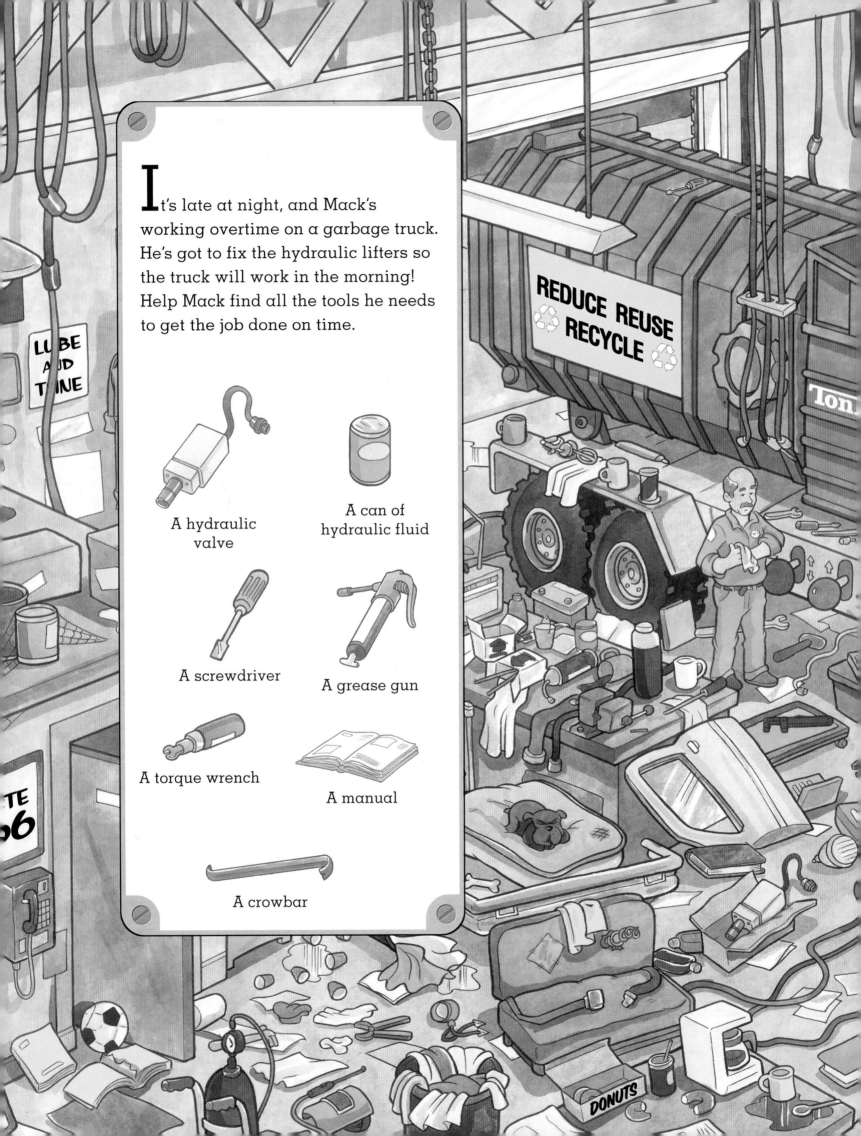

It's late at night, and Mack's working overtime on a garbage truck. He's got to fix the hydraulic lifters so the truck will work in the morning! Help Mack find all the tools he needs to get the job done on time.

A hydraulic valve

A can of hydraulic fluid

A screwdriver

A grease gun

A torque wrench

A manual

A crowbar

The dam has broken and the flood waters are rising! But the rescue helicopters, boats, and vehicles are rescuing folks as fast as they can. As fast as you can, search for and rescue these "R" things:

Really sleepy bear

Racoon

Ranger Roger

Rabbit

Rock climber

Red-tailed hawk

Rainbow trout

Rod & reel

Crystal
Lake
2 MILE
feet

In all the hurry and excitement of leaving the firehouse, some firemen left behind some important items. Can you find their forgotten gear?

- ☐ Rope
- ☐ Fireman Fred's badge
- ☐ Spark the Firedog's collar
- ☐ Fire Chief Williams's lucky yellow suspenders
- ☐ Watch
- ☐ Flashlight

All the policemen are practicing driving. Practice your detective skills by going back and finding these items.

- ☐ Binoculars
- ☐ Walkie talkie
- ☐ Box of donuts
- ☐ Book of mug shots
- ☐ Wanted poster for Boris Badguy
- ☐ Policemen's Ball tickets

Go back to the hospital construction site and use your keen sight to pick out all these things.

- ☐ Toolbox
- ☐ Wheelbarrow
- ☐ Hand saw
- ☐ A lost work glove
- ☐ Bubble-gum bubble
- ☐ Spilled cup of coffee

Oops! Everyone lost something in the crowds at the Air and Water Show. Return these things to their rightful owners.

- ☐ Pilot Jane's flight notebook
- ☐ Co-pilot Carl's sunglasses
- ☐ Otto-Pilot the Robot's oilcan
- ☐ Gary the Glider's propeller
- ☐ Harry the Hovercraft's anchor
- ☐ Captain Jack's life preserver
- ☐ Peg the Sea Dog's bone

Some farm animals escaped at the State Fair! Find them to return them to the safety of their pens.

☐ Cow
☐ Pig
☐ Horse
☐ Chicken
☐ Lamb
☐ Duck

Are we snow-blind, or seeing things? Look again in the storm for these shapes in the snow:

☐ A heart
☐ A star
☐ A cat
☐ A banana
☐ A fork and spoon
☐ A jack-o'-lantern
☐ An airplane

Mack's mechanic shop is too full! Help him clean up a bit by finding things that don't belong in his garage.

☐ Pineapple
☐ Women's shoes
☐ Surfboard
☐ Dolphin
☐ Soccer ball
☐ Eggbeater

On the Helicopter Rescue page, lots of people need rescuing from the rising waters, but don't forget to find and rescue some of our old friends from the previous pages.

☐ Spark the Firedog
☐ Officer O'Malley
☐ Foreman Smith
☐ Pilot Jane
☐ Otto-Pilot the Robot
☐ Farmer Howard
☐ Lacey
☐ Mechanic Mack